KU-018-475

Hayley Newman
Performancemania

[Including works by Malcolm&lily]

With an essay by Aaron Williamson

Matt's Gallery, London 2001

This publication has been produced on the occasion of Hayley Newman's
exhibition *The Daily Hayley* at Matt's Gallery, London 15–30 September 2001

Commissioned and published by Matt's Gallery
42-44 Copperfield Road, London E3 4RR
T: +44 (0)20 8983 1771, F: +44 (0)20 8983 1435
Director: Robin Klassnik
Gallery Administrator: Sarah den Dikken

Distributed by Cornerhouse Publications E: publications@cornerhouse.org

Copyright © Hayley Newman, Aaron Williamson & Matt's Gallery 2001

No part of this publication may be reproduced, copied or transmitted save with written permission from
the publisher, or in accordance with the provisions of the Copyright Designs & Patents Act, 1988

ISBN 0 907623 37 9

Matt's Gallery is a non-profit organisation. It is registered as a Friendly Society under the
Industrial & Provident Societies Act 1965. Registration number 27797
The gallery is financially supported by London Arts

Front and back cover photo: Hayley Newman *Suicide Cat*, 1995
Photo: Henner Winckler

709.2
NEW

Hayley Newman

26 0154784 0

Aaron Williamson

An introduction to Hayley Newman's *Performancemania*

The roots of contemporary performance can be traced back through two identifiable traditions. One leads back to traditional theatre, whilst also seeking its validation within contemporary post-structuralism. The centrality of theatrical principles is maintained, alongside the often arbitrary or gratuitous deployment of sensory-specific technology, such as video projectors, soundtracks and lighting. The other root of performance can be located in a fine art tradition which is anti-theatrical, discarding surface treatments and staging in order to place greater emphasis upon its three-dimensional (often public) setting. Such work sets out to vigorously interrogate its structure and materials for conceptual resonance.

Hayley Newman's allegiance is to this latter root of performance art, in sympathy with the European visual art Avant Garde, rather than the Anglo-American post-theatre sensibility. A post-graduate from London's Slade School of Art, her development has implied a rejection of mid 1990s British performance that, due to ingrained and political financial constraints had become increasingly accustomed to theatre/cabaret-style staging in nightclubs, bars and black-box studio theatres. Newman claimed in 1996 that she had left Britain for Germany in 1994 because the British performance scene had become increasingly theatre-based and that she wished to 'rediscover performance roots in Europe – Marina [Abramović] & Ulay, [Joseph] Beuys, Valie Export, Ulrike Rosenbach'.* Enrolling through a DAAD scholarship on Abramović's class in Germany, Newman's allegiance to the European Avant Garde makes her work unusual in the context of the 1990s British performance scene. The title of this book is only partly humorous. The term 'Performancemania' indicates that Newman is a longstanding enthusiast, or fan, of what she considers to be a genuinely revolutionary moment in art: the break both from theatrical performance and from object-based visual art, that can be recognised in the emergence of performance art in Europe during the 1960s and 1970s.

Newman's early works were concise investigations of specific materials and equipment. Her formal investigations of sound-making objects – such as hairdryers, records or microphones – was taken into the territory of politicised female subjectivity. A key work in this regard is *Microphone Skirt*, 1995, in which the erotic phallocentric and oral associations of the microphone are subsumed into making amplified sound when the microphones bash against each other in the 'microphone skirt'. The layering of sexual resonance is intense in this work, in which the body is 'skirted' by objects more usually associated with audio amplification and which here produce a rhythmic percussive sound. This resulting sound makes no claim for aesthetic achievement, but instead provides a slightly delayed rudimentary rhythm to which the performer's body may continue its rhythmic go-go dancing gyrations. The auto-eroticism of the act is pronounced and even finds an analogy when the microphones occasionally tip into a state of total feedback.

* See Antonia Hirsch, 'Hayley Newman Interview', *The Front Magazine*, Vancouver, 1996, p.10.

Several other works maintain this strategy of combining formal investigation of objects and equipment with more subjective associations. *Tour*, also from 1995, continues the exploration of the microphone as both object and sound generator, but this time presented as an isolated phallic instrument sellotaped to the groin in place of a guitar. Using a plectrum on the microphone's surface, Newman mimed along to rock music and the resulting click track effectively subverted a conventional masculine fantasy of libidinal power (the strutting air guitarist) by telescoping the raw sizeist insinuations of amplification and movement. Newman feminises the usually more masculine masturbatory actions of the air guitarist and as a result converts what is traditionally sexualised behaviour into purely performative qualities. The title, *Tour*, also indicates the rock star's fantasies of world domination, but Newman's tour was of a single building as she moved with her CD player and amp from room to room.

A similar pattern of ideas is taken into darker, more private territory with *Hook and Eye*, 1998. In place of the sexually objectified woman of *Microphone Skirt* and *Tour*, Newman's appearance in this piece is formally defined by her choice of material: a whole-body velcro suit that attaches to itself as she moves. Again using amplification, the mic'd up suit creates a mechanised, tearing sound that triggers a lightbulb making the performer momentarily visible. Again, the associative layering is intense but with an emphasis which seems to imply that the body's relationship to pure visibility (or light) is one of friction and laborious manufacture rather than weightless appearance.

Whereas many of Newman's pieces involve formal investigation of sensory information – through sound and lighting – she has also on occasion made works that more specifically explore the interaction and definition of both the viewer and performer. In *Suicide Cat*, 1995, Newman lay prostrate, face down, on the ground at the entrance to a public building. Her pose and what she wore – fake fur coat and mask – was that of a big game rug. The animal's tail though, continued to rotate comically as members of the public stepped around the rug to enter or leave the building. The image is cartoon-like – a cat landed splat on the floor, perhaps through suicide as the title indicates – but the piece also provided the visitors to the building with an all too noticeable intervention, providing a confrontation, emphasising an environment where nature is flattened by concrete. The animal/human theme was also addressed by Newman in the same year with *Kalte Schulter* in which Newman was delivered to a gathering at a gallery, dressed in a polar bear suit and wrapped in Cellophane. Reminiscent of a sport mascot or a high street leafleter, Newman's animal impersonation punctured the laboured seriousness of the gallery audience by exploiting the curious sentimentalism that humans have towards their neutered, yet anthropomorphic, representations of animals. Here though, after a cuddlesome and accommodating welcome, after the cellophane wrapping had been peeled away, the beast emerged as Newman began expressing sexual aggression towards the bear's human admirers.

Alongside Newman's development of solo pieces, she has placed an equal emphasis on working collaboratively with a number of other artists. Chief among these (and documented in this book) are her works with Nina Könnemann, operating under the name Malcolm&lily. With a foundation in friendship, this collaboration seems to have afforded each artist a forum in which to explore more irreverent, nervy and spontaneous works. Newman and Könnemann's collaborative pieces exemplify both the experimental condition and mandate of performance art in that they were conceived and executed fairly spontaneously, requiring immediate decisions to act on irreverent, urgent ideas. In *World of Sex*, 1995, the performers sleepwalk, arms aloft, through Hamburg's red-light district on a full moon, contrasting the surrounding sexual commerce with the pantomime of trash Zombie flicks. The titular *Delta*, 1995, was derived from the artists' urine mingling as they 'competitively piss on the posh side of town', watering the walkways of the straight-laced with the transgressive fluency of childhood games on skid row. In *Old Fashioned Paradise*, 1995, a chauffeur drove Newman and Könnemann around Hamburg as they both sat naked in the back of an open-top cabriolet. Their occasional mimicking of glamorous postures was a celebration of alfresco living, of the Edenic luxury of being unadorned in the midst of the city's stressed-out traffic system. Twice during the performance the car was stopped, the artists cautioned and forced by uniformed police to cover themselves up.

The reverse orders, visual layering and paradoxes of much of the work made by Newman in Hamburg in 1995 were in many ways preparation for the work that she conceived as a deconstructive commentary upon one of the key elements in both her identity and public presentation of herself as a performance artist. Observing that the spontaneity of performance and its communication through imagery was dependent to a large degree on the possibility of its documentation, she began to address 'the problem of how to represent the work beyond the moment, or […] whether to represent that moment at all.'* Furthermore, she began to query 'what type of performance communicates best through the image?', noting that many performances 'have not made the translation into the single image'. Proposing that the use of imagery 'is antithetical to the "real" event', Newman conceived a work that would subvert the processes by which performance works (often attended by very few people) are distributed to the many through publications consisting of documentary images and accompanying descriptive texts. With the resulting series of false documents of faked performances entitled *Connotations – Performance Images 1994–98*, Newman was able to resolve her earlier feelings towards the dichotomy of fine art and theatre performance by creating her own theatre of performance documentation.

Connotations … is as much a homage as it is a critique of classic performance art and its search for authenticity in the face of a sterile, self-simulating world. And yet, all of the texts and the images which taken together make up *Connotations* … are staged fakes of the performances they describe and illustrate. That is, not only are the images carefully and artificially staged, but the texts also describe circumstances that equally do not pertain to what the images appear to show. *Connotations* … is a hall of mirrors in which dates, times, locations, media and audiences are all insistently invented or faked. In this way, the potency of performance art – its veneer of authenticity, however extraordinary the events described might be – is decontextualised and subjected to the kind of interven-

* This and the following quotes are taken from Hayley Newmans unpublished notes for the *Connotations* … project.

tions that are concerns within all the other forms of contemporary image making. Indeed, it seems extraordinary that it has taken so long for the genre of performance documentation to be subjected to the kind of deconstructive strategies that have been routinely applied within other contemporary art practices.

The possibility of delivering a work that is unmediated in terms of the relationship between self (artist) and society (material) was one of the major concerns of classic performance art; the difficulty being inherently obvious when faced with the impossibility of representation being carried out in terms of a practice which embraces that which is up to a point unmediated. In a media-saturated world, strategies of representation are refractory forms of collateral – our cultural overlords – and performance art, with its roots in a dematerialised and non-commodified art making, can often be read as a sustained opposition to representation. Not least, this opposition has to be understood in terms of the idealised immediacy of visual imagery being replaced in performance by the three-dimensionality of an event. Most performance artists, whilst emphasising the primacy of an unrepresentable dimension of the physical event nonetheless engage with methods of documenting it, creating a representation through one form (video, photos, recordings, written descriptions) or another. In this perhaps intrinsically self-contradictory way performance art has facilitated its own commodification as sets of histories, disseminated in the form of 'drive-by' publications that combine the iconic image with the pithy, all-encompassing, caption.

It is here that Newman, with her *Connotations ...* series intervenes into the complex dynamics that performance art explores. A selection from the series was exhibited in 2000 at London's ICA alongside a notice stating that the works were all faked. However, many newspapers published accounts of the *Connotations ...* pieces as if Newman had actually performed them in the ways that the captions describe. This response wilfully ignored the subtleties of her statement in favour of anecdotal sensationalism.* This could even be taken to indicate that the media are, within the constraints of journalism, perhaps unwilling to represent the problem of representation itself. Or rather, where the media often exhibit a self-obsession with their own manipulations and distortions, they simultaneously avoid revealing the means by which they sustain these strategies, so that their cultural authority is upheld. In contrast to the media, however, performance art is precisely predicated upon this analysis and this is why Newman's *Connotations ...* sequence is simultaneously both a critique and a work of performance art. Her strategy is not one of distancing irony but of an embracing deconstruction. Indeed, the self-reflexivity that is proposed and exploited by *Connotations ...* is such that it may lay claim to having collapsed the traditional nexus between work and documentation by inventing documentation as a work in itself.

For performance documentation, images are often produced using whatever convenient tools are at hand – video, Polaroids, snapshot cameras, hastily scrawled notes, preparatory sketches – which are all subsumed into the aura of revealing an actual, unique and, by implication, extraordinary event. This dynamic is central to Newman's *Connotations ...* The images deliberately subvert their own transparency by being essentially and painstakingly falsified; they are unrelentingly

* See especially, *The Times*, 2 February 2000; *Time Out*, 22 March; *The Sunday Herald*, 19 March; *The Observer*, 26 March; *Evening Standard*, 16 & 17 March; *The Guardian*, 21 March; as well as several smaller newspapers. This misreporting continued even after Newman restated in the *Evening Standard* on 16 March, that the works were faked. Indeed, the same newspaper carried reports on 16 & 17 March that continued to describe the work as depicting real events. The exhibition at the ICA was part of the *Beck's Futures* art competition in April 2000.

9

untrue to the circumstances by which they are baldly described in accompanying texts. The frame of the work, however, does not show any glimpse of this artifice, everything rings true as the image of a plausible performance, occasionally to the point of being almost pedantically convincing. Nonetheless, Newman has invented extraordinary, quixotic and rarefied concepts entirely separated from any intended performance other than to manufacture an image that will serve to illustrate the idea.

It is a part of performance art's *frisson* that any photographic image of a rarefied and unique, extraordinary occurrence (often only sparsely witnessed by the public), is by implication a bonus to the fact that such a thing occurred. There are no photographs, say, of Gérard de Nerval walking a lobster at the end of a blue ribbon through the gardens of the Palais Royal in Paris in the 1850s, although such an image is just about historically possible. In the absence of an image the imagination may experience a craving for any dubious blurred document upon which to project intensity, integrity and an elevated sense of the eventful extraordinary moment. Such a document also provides historians with the evidence they require to prove such an event took place. Likewise, Newman neutralises the quality of technical achievement that her imagery in *Connotations…* may convey in order to appear to be residual to the (fictive) historic moment. One piece is pointedly designed to illustrate this question of rarity/neutrality: the caption to *Stealth* states that 'prior to the event I had instructed its organiser to enter at any point during the three hour performance and take a single photograph […] this is the only image of the work as no other photography was allowed.'

In fact, none of the stated conditions for this or any of the other pieces are to be taken at surface value. The subtitle of the series is itself misleading,* rather than being *Performance Images* from the period 1994–98, the photographs were mostly taken during one week. Newman created an elaborate system of visual continuity in order to authenticate the four year period so that where fictional dates are close to each other she has a similar hairstyle and her clothing is adapted to the fictional season. Dates and venues are also falsified according to varying personal significance such as family birthdays and places Newman had visited. Even the selection of film format, type of film and print quality was carefully made to authenticate the premise that the photographs were taken over a four year period. The intention to fabricate a four year career of performances takes on further resonance within the pages of this book as the *Connotations …* images are paradoxically afforded camouflage by the surrounding documentation of Newman's actual performances.

Part of this elaborate fiction was to imitate the character of much performance photo-documentation that is seemingly produced ad hoc, appearing functionally achieved and non-showy. Printed mostly in black and white – that traditionally upheld carrier of photographic authenticity – there is however a careful compositional construction at work in many of the photographs. *Crying Glasses (An Aid to Melancholia)*, for example, uses Adrian Piper's documentary photograph of her performance *Catalysis IV*, 1970, as a form of palimpsest. Piper's image shows her seated on a bus with a towel stuffed inside her mouth as a woman passenger

* The original title of the work specified the period 1994–98 but has since been abbreviated.

wearing Jackie Onassis-style sunglasses turns away in disapproval.* Newman similarly uses the framing of her photograph to portray the disapproval (masquerading as studied indifference) of a fellow passenger, half hiding behind a newspaper as Newman apparently pumps tears through her Onassis-style sunglasses. The caption for this piece states that Newman performed this action 'over a year' and that it was conceived 'to enable the representation of feelings in public spaces'. Naturally, this photograph is in fact of a single, staged event and the tears were wiped on glycerine. Yet whereas the photograph affords Newman a resonant image that powerfully enacts a dialogue with Piper's *Catalysis IV*, it is the conceptual apparatus between image and caption that is the true composition of the piece. This factor is apparent in the piece entitled *Bass in a Space*. Here, a somewhat rudimentary photograph of a hand pointing to a crack in the wall is accompanied by a caption claiming that the crack appeared after playing low frequencies over a PA in a room 'inversely proportional to the size of the PA'. Several of the *Connotations …* defy credibility (where others are easily believed) but the detail of the caption seems to deliberately stretch the plausibility of the image's reading. Rather than simply being a joke, this narrative of stretched credibility is in fact right at the heart of performance documentation's power of dissemination.

As one example, Chris Burden has represented *Five day locker piece*, 1971,‡ with a terse description of being imprisoned in a small locker for five consecutive days. His text is accompanied by a somewhat banal photograph of a locker. Can we be sure that Chris Burden is inside it? In relation to Burden's performance documentation, Newman (in the 'Self-Interview' on pages 83–91) suggests 'that a visual document […] and text […] are being used to authorise one another and that in their collusion they are self-reflexive.' Going from the purely visual information of Burden's photograph there is no absolute proof of the truth of his testimony and we have to trust that an artist would not go to the lengths that Newman has done in order to fabricate a lie. Or rather, in order to reveal that in performance documentation an image does not, in itself, encapsulate a concept.

This principle is emphasised in many of the other *Connotations …* pieces, so that, increasingly suspicious, the viewer becomes more aware of what the images actually show rather than what the captions tell. Photographs of a binliner bag beside a pile of rubbish (*B[in]*), a busker on the street (*Exploding LEGO*), a pile of inflated sandwich bags (*Human Resources*), a record with holes drilled into it (*Occasionally Groovy*) are each accompanied by dizzying, involved narratives in order to locate them as works of performance art. *Football Audio Cup* converts photographs of a simple kickabout into a record of an intriguing conceptual performance that is readily pictured in the imagination – if only it had happened in the way described. The fiction in this piece extends to listing two teams comprised of Newman's friends, only some of whom were present at the event, and yet the basic data that the piece claims to be inspired by – the football match, its circumstances, result and scorer – are all true.

It is this destabilising of the viewer's position that accounts for much of the power of *Connotations …* Many visitors to the exhibition of selected pieces from the series at London's ICA may have attempted to gain some purchase on

* A photograph of Adrian Piper's *Catalysis IV* can be found in Adrian Piper, *Out of Order, Out of Sight, Selected Writings in Meta-Art, 1968-1992*, Vol. I, MIT Press, 1996, p.43.

‡ See *Chris Burden*, Blocnotes Editions, Paris, 1995, p.22. The original text, in English, is printed on p.127.

performance art itself prior to realising the further tortuous twist that these elaborate works are all in fact faked. Although Yves Klein faked his *Leap into the Void*, 1960, montage photograph, the resulting image was underpinned by the artist's own ambitiously heroic persona. In contrast, many of Newman's photographs fake the circumstances described and depicted to greater degrees of intricacy only in order to create further layers of artifice as critique. This strategy, rather than representing a secondary ironic position, in fact takes Newman further into a primary intent. This is because her intervention brings performance art closer to itself and is truer to the dynamics and problematics upon which it was founded. Specifically, *Connotations* … takes us further into performance's legacy of opposition to the commodifiable object which, as Newman shows, the iconic images which make up performance history ultimately and inevitably are.

After *Connotations* … Newman began to explore shifting the ground of documentation from the photograph to other media such as writing, sound generation and physical trace. In *Kiss Exam* and *A Translation of the Sensation of the Left Hand into the Right*, both 1999, the formal possibility of documenting through writing became the actual physical activity of the performance. In both these works Newman investigated her own sensations (of kissing someone and of placing a hand in butter) by writing them out live. *A Translation of the Sensation of the Left Hand into the Right* articulates a materialist position in which writing remains close to the physical circumstances of its production. The materialism is also pronounced in the sculptural sense that butter, through the conduit of the artist's translation from one hand to the other, is alchemically converted into ink. This quality of translation and transformation is also the key process at the heart of Newman's *Soundgaze*, 1999, this time from objects into sound. The weight of an object or a combination of objects, when placed on an electronic weighing scale, triggers off pre-programmed sounds ascribed to that specific weight. The performance allows Newman to construct intricate patterns of material equivalence (of texture, volume and quality) between the programmed sounds and the visual properties of the objects. Newman's own persona in this piece is somewhere between orchestrator and warehouse labourer as the objects and their accompanying sounds are apprehended by the audience.

Thinking, 2000, is also concerned with transformation, this time through the communication of a series of ideas to a solo performer, whose responses to thinking the idea are observed by the audience. A subtle and complex work, *Thinking* is a meditation on the intrinsic empiricism that underpins communication. Newman (who was not present at the performance) recited through headphones a list of over 250 instructions for the performer to think about, such as 'walking round a shopping centre with a plastic bag over your left foot'.* The performer visibly followed the curves of language to arrive at the thought. Although the audience does not hear Newman's spoken suggestions, they are able to read them from a sheet of paper that states the times at which the performer will be thinking them. Hence, her responses, rendered utterly untheatrically by the performer – such as wry smiles, blankness, giggling, puzzlement, boredom, – are facially registered as the substance of the transformative process. Newman's suggested thoughts are

* The full list of instructions for *Thinking* can be found in Hayley Newman, *Locating Performance: Textual Identity and the Performative*, unpublished PhD thesis, University of Leeds, 2001.

designed (sometimes through outrageousness, other times through obliqueness or even banality) to provoke from both the performer and, by extension, the audience responses that construct performance as a self-conscious event.

It is through such strategies in Newman's later work that she continues to develop and evolve the parameters of contemporary performance art. Her critique of the iconic performance image in *Connotations* ... seems to have led her into increasingly open-ended structures that emphasise the transient, multi-focal quality of performance. It is as if her work proliferates at the edges of any one position, spreading out to efface the centrality of either the performer or the audience in order to intensify each's tacit contribution. She proposes the viewer or listener as an active component, continuing to disperse performance in as many directions as possible and for as far as it can go.

Record
1994

A record pressed with the sound of my own voice singing an 'Ooh', the sound of which was sampled to produce a continuous tone that was modulated over an octave in pitch. In the performance I wore three pick-up styli attached to the fingers of my right hand. I played the record, accessing it from more than one point at any given time.

Record 29 May 1994, Nosepaint, London; *Record* plus *Microphone Skirt*, *Crystalline II* and *Shot in the Dark* 19 October 1997, 'Nacht-Schräge', Spiel.Art '97, Munich.

Photo (work in progress): Christina Lamb

Kiss
1994

A performed kiss that took place on a night club balcony at midnight. In the performance a microphone, passed between two mouths, amplifies the unseen movement of two mouths kissing.

Kiss 29 May 1994, Nosepaint, London.

Photos courtesy of Nosepaint

Ecomiss
1994
Using mountaineering equipment, I am photographed climbing on the board-room table of *The Economist* magazine.

Ecomiss 22 June – 13 July 1994, 'The Economist Ninth Annual Summer Exhibition', The Economist Building, London.

Photo: Christina Lamb

Kalte Schulter
1995

Delivered to the gallery wrapped in
cellophane and dressed as a polar bear
I carry a lollipop with the message 'Love
me' written on it. Once unwrapped I
have my photo taken with people before
turning sexually aggressive towards
them.

Kalte Schulter 12 May 1995, 'Bild Me, Bild You',
Gallerie KM25, Hamburg.

Photo: Henner Winckler

Microphone Skirt

1995

Erotic go-go dancing in a skirt made from 20 hi-ball mikes. As I moved, the microphones hung around my waist jostled and knocked against each other, tracing my physical movements with sound.

Microphone Skirt 19 May 1995, 'ImPure', Osterwalder's Art Office, Hamburg; *Microphone Skirt* 10 & 12 November 1995, 'The Tingle Factor', Hoog Huis, Arnhem; *Microphone Skirt* 24 April 1996, The Savage Club, Manchester; *Microphone Skirt* 28 March 1996, 'The British Ambience', Tresor, Berlin; *Microphone Skirt* 7 September 1996, at the opening for *Rude Mechanic*, Beaconsfield, London; *Microphone Skirt* plus *Shot in the Dark* 3 October 1996, 'Visionfest', The V-Club, Liverpool; *Microphone Skirt* plus *Crystalline II*, *Shot in the Dark* and *Record*, 19 October 1997, 'Nacht-Schräge', Spiel.Art '97, Munich.

Photo: Ewjenia Tsanana

Suicide Cat

1995

Wearing a pair of false teeth, a cats mask, cats ears and a leopardskin coat with a rotating tail sewn into its back, I lie on the floor impersonating a colonial rug.

Suicide Cat June 1995, Hochschule für Bildende Künste, Hamburg; *Suicide Cat* 13 & 14 August 1997, 'Between the Devil and the Deep (Blue) Sea', Muu/Beaconsfield, Helsinki.

Photo: Riikka Makinen

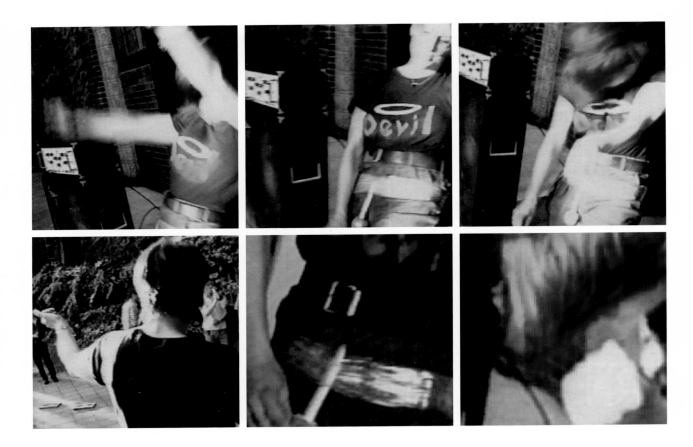

Tour

1995

A portable performance made to be performed as many times as possible. In the performance I wear a microphone strapped around my waist with Sellotape, which I play with a plectrum like an air guitar. Each performance lasted the length of a track playing back on a CD player.

Tour June 1995, Hochschule für Bildende Künste, Hamburg; *Tour* June 1995, Rote Flora, Hamburg; *Tour* 29 March 1996, 'The British Ambience', Podewill, Berlin.

Video stills

16 6 1995

That's Why They're Doing It

In collaboration with Nina Könnemann
as Malcolm&lily
1995
A begging happening and burlesque
show on the U-Bahn in Berlin.

That's Why They're Doing It 16 June 1995, U-Bahn,
Berlin.

Video still

World of Sex

In collaboration with Nina Könnemann
as Malcolm&lily
1995
Sleepwalking along the Reeperbahn in
Hamburg at full moon.

World of Sex, July 1995, Reeperbahn, Hamburg.

Video still

Delta

In collaboration with Nina Könnemann
as Malcolm&lily
1995
Competitive pissing on the posh side
of town.

Delta July 1995, Blankenese, Hamburg

Video stills

Old Fashioned Paradise

In collaboration with Nina Könnemann
as Malcolm&lily
1995
Naked in a chauffeur driven cabriolet.

Old Fashioned Paradise, July 1995, Hamburg.

Photographer unknown

Invisible Crowds

1996

A video installation based on a performance in which 50 people get on and off a BC transit bus in Vancouver, Canada.

Filmed in real time from the back seat of the bus, one video shows a crowd of volunteers travelling around Vancouver in a bus. When the bus stops the crowd exits and the vehicle continues its journey, empty until it returns to pick up the waiting crowd and begin the cycle again.

The second video in the installation shows a close-up of the spools of a reel to reel tape recorder moving round as it plays a soundtrack of people talking when the crowd is on the bus, and pausing motionless and silent after they leave.

Invisible Crowds 6 February – 3 March 1996, The Western Front, Vancouver, Canada.
Photo: Reece Rehm Metcalf

Shot in the Dark

1996

A light sensitive dress is illuminated by a professional flash unit. The flash unit is triggered by a miked-up camera, which provides a mechanistic soundtrack to the performance. The performance takes place in the dark. As the flash is triggered, the sound of the amplified camera mechanism is heard and I am seen for a moment, after which the glowing image of the dress remains hovering in space. In the optical after-image I appear to be disembodied, floating, head separated from body, legs separated from torso, arms from chest.

Performance history overleaf.

Shot in the Dark 25 June 1996, 'Geben und nehmen', Schloß Plüschow, Mecklenburg; Shot in the Dark 6 & 7 September 1996, 'Club Foot', Extrapool, Nijmegen; Shot in the Dark 2 October 1996, 'Visionfest', Atkinson Art Gallery & Museum, Southport; Shot in the Dark plus Microphone Skirt 3 October 1996, 'Visionfest', The V-Club, Liverpool; Shot in the Dark 14 November 1996, 'Sin Número Arte de Acción', Circulo de Bellas Artes, Festivales de Madrid; Shot in the Dark and performance with Bruce Gilchrist 25 January 1997, Hollywood Leather, London; Shot in the Dark 11 April 1997, 'Zero Gravity', Videopositive; Shot in the Dark 12 July 1997, 'Soundproofs', Museum of Installation, London; Shot in the Dark plus Microphone Skirt, Crystalline II and Record 19 October 1997, 'Nacht-Schräge', Spiel.Art '97, Munich; Shot in the Dark plus Hook and Eye and Crystalline II 18 April 1998, 'Méta femmes br@nchées', Studio XX, Montreal; Shot in the Dark plus Hook and Eye and Crystalline II 14 October 1998, 'Re-Inventing the Diva', The Western Front, Vancouver; Shot in the Dark plus Hook and Eye and Crystalline II 23 October 1998, 'Dimenzió Ugrás', Trafó Galeria, Budapest; Shot in the Dark and Crystalline II, 16 January 1999, 'Small Pleasures', 'Sensation', Berlin; Shot in the Dark plus Hook and Eye 7 September 1999, 'Dislocation', hARTware projekte, Dortmund.

Photo: Chris Hewitt

Rude Mechanic

In collaboration with David Crawforth and Pan Sonic
1996

Rude Mechanic was a month long collaboration between myself, David Crawforth, Finnish sound duo Pan Sonic and various invited musicians. The project, set up as an exploration of the relationship between sound and vision, located both performers and musicians within a symbiotic relationship in which the visual was urged on by the audio and the audio by the visual.

Rude Mechanic, 9 November – 7 December 1996, Beaconsfield, London.

Photo courtesy of Beaconsfield

Crystalline I, II & III

1997

Crystalline was performed in different ways over a two year period. In all examples of the performance I wore a pair of stiletto shoes with motors inserted into their heels and either stood on or leaned against a miked-up surface. *Crystalline I* was performed lying on the floor with my feet resting against a vertical plane, *Crystalline II* while standing on a hard surface, such as a table-top whilst in *Crystalline III* I was suspended above that plane. In each performance the vibrations made by the motors in the shoes were amplified through their contact with a miked-up surface.

Crystalline I originally in the series *Four Performance Sketches* 27 February 1997, 'One Night Stand', Norwich Art Gallery, Norwich; *Crystalline I* 28 June 1997, 'Performa '97', Gallerie Barbara Thumm, Berlin; *Crystalline II* as a part of the series of performances titled 'Four Weeks Without Crutches, 14–31 August 1997, 'Between the Devil and the Deep (Blue) Sea', Esplanade Bandstand, Helsinki; *Crystalline II* plus *Microphone Skirt*, *Shot in the Dark* and *Record* 19 October 1997, 'Nacht Schräge', Spiel.Art '97, Munich; *Crystalline II* 25 October 1997, 'Sprawl–Compass', The Cockpit Theatre, London; *Crystalline III* 20 May 1998, 'Tolv Netter', Kulturhueset USF, Bergen; *Crystalline II* plus *Hook and Eye* and *Shot in the Dark* 18 April 1998, 'Méta femmes br@nchées', Studio XX, Montreal; *Crystalline II* plus *Hook and Eye* and *Shot in the Dark* 14 October 1998, 'Re-Inventing the Diva', The Western Front, Vancouver; *Crystalline II* plus *Hook and Eye* and *Shot in the Dark* 23 October 1998, 'Dimenzió Ugrás', Trafó Galeria, Budapest. *Crystalline II* plus *Hook and Eye* 24 October 1998,

The Rhiz, Vienna; *Crystalline II* plus *Hook and Eye* 22 December 1998, 'Chain Gang', Strike, London; *Crystalline II* plus *Shot in the Dark* 16 January 1999, 'Small Pleasures', 'Sensation' , Hamburger Bahnhof, Berlin; *Crystalline II* plus *Hook and Eye* with Matt Wand, 2 July 1999, '33'' 45'' 78'' '99', Kulturzentrum 'd Zuckerfabrik, Enns.

Photos (*Crystalline I*): Kirk Laws-Chapman

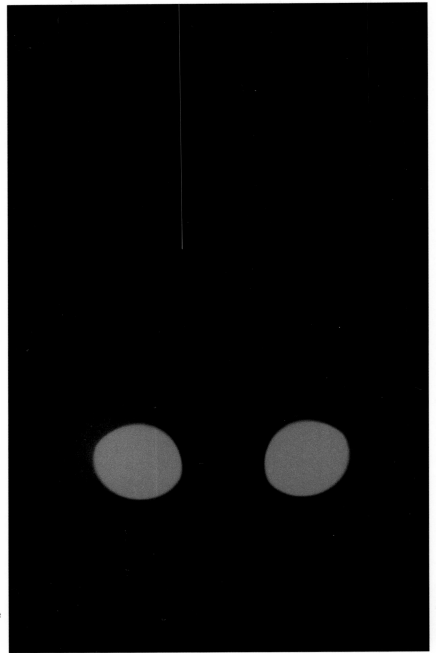

Endless Loop

In collaboration with Robert Ellis
1997

Night. An open air car park without
light. A black car. Its headlights are on.
The bonnet and boot are both open.
The engine is stuffed with tape-
recorders that play the sound of bird-
song. In the boot a man quietly reads
poetry by torchlight. Two microphones
are placed on stands at either end of the
car park. The surface is gravel. I slowly
drive the car backwards and forwards
between the two microphones. The microphones alternately amplify the
spaces of the boot and the bonnet. The
car displaces the gravel.

Endless Loop, 21 March 1997, 'Young Parents', The
Annual Progamme: No.3 Riverside Mews,
Manchester.

Photo: Brian Crawford

Overleaf

Donnerwetter

**In collaboration with Nina Könnemann
as Malcolm&lily
1997**
A miniature thunderstorm on the
streets of Berlin. The thunderstorm
comprised of three elements: a hose
pipe with a spray attachment (rain), a
metal thunderboard (thunder) and a
Polaroid camera (lightning). Passers-by
were invited to stand under an umbrella
for their personalised weather
experience.

Donnerwetter 28 June 1997, 'Performa '97',
Gallerie Barbara Thumm, Berlin.

Polaroids: Nina Könnemann

44/60

45/60

46/60

47/60

34

Hook and Eye
1998

A performance in the dark wearing a full body suit made from velcro with a series of 14 microphones sewn inside it. As I move the sound of velcro sticking against itself is amplified. A sound to light unit translates the noise of the Velcro into an electrical pulse, which in turn illuminates a single 200W bulb. I am only seen when I move.

Hook and Eye 24 January 1998, 'Ron ton tonnie', De Fabriek, Eindhoven; *Hook and Eye* 27 February 1998, 'No-tech', Podewill, Berlin; *Hook and Eye* plus *Shot in the Dark* and *Crystalline II* 18 April 1998, 'Méta femmes br@nchées', Studio XX, Montreal; *Hook and Eye* 23 April 1998, 'The Tingle Factor', ICA, London; *Hook and Eye* 22 May 1998, 'Tolv Netter', Kulturhueset USF, Bergen; *Hook and Eye* 9 October 1998, 'Lucid', ROOT '98; *Hook and Eye* plus *Shot in the Dark* and *Crystalline II* 14 October 1998, 'Re-Inventing the Diva', The Western Front, Vancouver; *Hook and Eye* plus *Crystalline II* and *Shot in the Dark* 23 October 1998, 'Dimenzió Ugrás', Trafó Galeria, Budapest; *Hook and Eye* plus *Crystalline II* 24 October 1998, The Rhiz, Vienna; *Hook and Eye* plus *Crystalline II* 22 December 1998, 'Chain Gang', Strike, London; *Hook and Eye* 10 April 1999, 'Performance Index', Museum of Architecture, Basel; *Hook and Eye* 16 April 1999, 'Link', Prato Museum of Modern Art, Prato; *Hook and Eye* and *Crystalline II* with Matt Wand, 2 July 1999, '33" 45" 78" '99', Kulturzentrum 'd Zuckerfabrik, Enns; *Hook and Eye* plus *Shot in the Dark* 7 September 1999, 'Dislocation', hARTware projekte, Dortmund.

Photo: Jan Poloczek

Flea Circus

In collaboration with Nina Könnemann
as Malcolm&lily
1998
Individual audience members were invited to sit at a table and through a large magnifying glass view a scene from the Beckett play *Waiting for Godo,* in this miniature flea theatre. In the scene, two fleas (with sunflower seeds for bodies and garlic skin for wings) attached to coat hanger wire hovered around a tomato stalk. Once the audience member was seated, Nina and I positioned ourselves to whisper Didi and Gogo's lines into his or her ears, simultaneously manipulating the movements of the two fleas.

Flea Circus 28 February 1998, 'No-tech' festival, Podewill, Berlin.

Photo: (preparing for the performance)
Nina Könnemann

Human Resources I

1998

Overnight, I decorated the Fine Art
office at the University of Leeds with
stationery. The next day, unannounced,
the department secretary worked in the
office dressed as a fly.

Human Resources I with Jane Czyzselska,
University of Leeds, Fine Art Department, May
1998.

Photo: Lisa Watts

Connotations – Performance Images

The photographs in the series *Connotations – Performance Images* are constructed fictional images intended to explore the role of documentation in performance. The photographs in the series were staged and performed by myself with most of the photographs being taken by the photographer Casey Orr over a week in the summer of 1998. The dates, locations, photographers and contexts for the performances cited in the text panels are fictional. In all instances the action had to be performed for the photograph but did not take place within the circumstances, time or place outlined in the supporting text.

As a form, performance is often mediated through the documentary image, video, film, text or by word of mouth and rumour. With so few existing networks for the distribution of performance works, it is the image and its supporting text that is given privilege in publications on the subject, creating a handful of historical performances that have become notorious through their own documentation, leaving others behind that have not made the translation into the single image.

Connotations – Performance Images was made as a way to understand how the documentary performance image works in relation to text, as well as creating the context to make work for which there was, at that time, no practical forum. The images chosen for this series of documents aim to evoke ideas beyond photography and reflect the ambiguity implicit in attempts to document (capture) a performance within a photograph. The document replaces the performance: the camera authenticates the activity in its position as witness and the photographic image stands in place of the performance and becomes the work itself. When supported by other information such as dates, location, and use of materials, duration and description of events these images can provide the forensic link to communicate ideas that occurred within the live performance to a non-live situation.

Connotations – Performance Images is an ongoing project.

Connotations – Performance Images 1994–98: 10–25 October 1998, Beverley Art Gallery, Beverley; *Connotations – Performance Images*, 9–10 July 1999, 'Home 2', Home, London; *Connotations – Performance Images*, 17 March – 17 May 2000, 'Beck's Futures', ICA, London (selection of works); *Connotations – Performance Images* 26 May – 2 July 2000, 'Beck's Futures', Cornerhouse, Manchester (selection of works); *Connotations – Performance Images*, 16 September – 14 October 2000, 'Beck's Futures', CCA, Glasgow (selection of works); *Connotations – Performance Images*, 1 February – 29 April 2001, 'Century City: Art and Culture in the Modern Metropolis', Tate Modern, London (selection of works).

All *Connotations* … photographs are editions of three.

I-Spy Surveillance Fly

July, 1994

Social Security Offices, Amsterdam, Holland, as a part of the exhibition 'Implant', organised by Arts Projects Europe. Photo: Thomas Peutz
Colour R-Type photographic print
30·2 × 30·2 cm

Over the duration of a week I sat dressed as a fly, wearing a pair of customised glasses in different vantage points around the social security offices in Amsterdam. The glasses, which had two miniature surveillance cameras attached, relayed a live stereoscopic image to a single monitor placed in the offices' waiting room. No video recordings were made. My movements were constantly monitored by staff.

25th Birthday Party

18 November 1994

Hamburg. Photo: Nina Könnemann
Black & white photographic print 40 × 26·7cm

Crying Glasses (An Aid to Melancholia)

1995

On public transport in Hamburg, Berlin, Rostock, London and Guildford. Photo; Christina Lamb
Black & white photographic print 40·2 × 50·2cm

Over a year I wore the crying glasses while travelling on public transport in all the cities I visited. The glasses functioned using a pump system which, hidden inside my jacket, allowed me to pump water up out of the glasses and produce a trickle of tears down my cheeks. The glasses were conceived as a tool to enable the representation of feelings in public spaces. Over the months of wearing the glasses they became an external mechanism which enabled the manifestation of internal and unidentifiable emotions.

Electric Strip

12 April 1995

'Kleidung', All Girls Gallery, Berlin.
Photo: Nina Könnemann
Colour C-Type photographic print 30·7 × 29 cm

Standing on two dinner plates while wearing 20 nylon petticoats with positive and negative electrical cables attached to my legs. Audiences of no more than five people were led into the semi-lit room, where I instructed them to stand as close to me as possible. The performance started as someone wound a hand winch, creating a small electric charge through my body. As I began to remove the nylon petticoats, static electricity darted between the layers of nylon effecting an intimate light show.

Spirit

31 October 1995

Soho, London. Photo: Kerry Baldry
Digital colour print 59 × 83·5 cm

Dressed as a ghost for Halloween I ran into various pubs in London's Soho, stole a drink and then left.

Virtual Techno Sponge

17 January 1996

Live video link between my studio in London
and The Western Front, Vancouver
Colour photocopy 25 × 39·5 cm

Robert Fillou celebrated the birth of art
by placing a sponge into a bucket. Since
then various Fluxus affiliated organisa-
tions across the world have annually
celebrated Art's birthday. *Virtual Techno
Sponge* was part of a live video-confer-
ence hosted by The Western Front in
Vancouver, Canada, to which I con-
tributed the act of shutting a sponge
in the door of my studio.

B(in)

14 April 1996

New York. Photographer unknown
Black & white photographic print 39 × 39 cm

Sitting in a bin bag waiting for bin men
to pick me up in New York. When the
bin men arrived at 4pm, I jumped out of
the bag and ran home.

Meditation on Gender Difference

21 July 1996

Lexham Gardens, London.
Photo: Christina Lamb
Colour C-Type print 40 × 26·7cm

For the work I made a suit which, acting like an inverted bikini, entirely covered the body except for the genital and chest areas. I sat in the garden at home all day wearing the suit, only removing the inverted bikini in the early evening to reveal sunburn on the areas of the body which are normally concealed and protected. In the work the body itself articulates emotion through a controlled physical reaction expressed in the form of intense sunburn.

Stealth

22 November 1996

Ave, Arnhem. Photo: Alphonse Ter Avest
Black & white photographic print 55 × 106 cm

Over 3 hours I jumped up and down on a trampoline in complete darkness. A small flashing red light attached to my body and the sound of my movements were the only two things indicative of any activity.

Prior to the event I had instructed its organiser to enter at any point during the three hour long performance and take a single photograph with a flash to document the work. This is the only image of the work as no other photography was allowed.

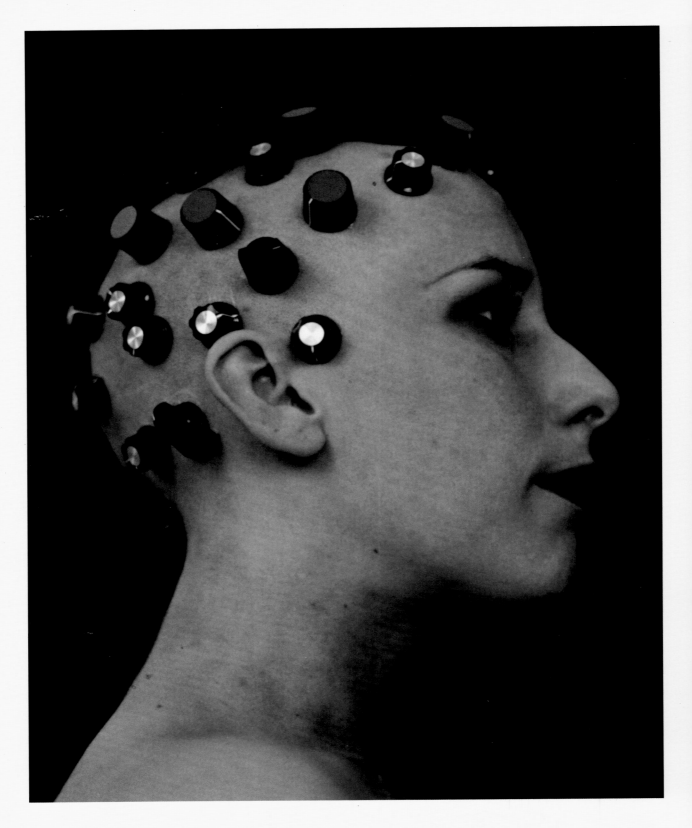

Head

Studio photograph 1997

Photo opposite: Casey Orr
Black & white photographic print 92·5 × 91 cm

Page 54

You Blew My Mind

Studio photograph 1997

Photo: Casey Orr
Black & white photographic print 92·5 × 91 cm

Page 55

Blow Out

Studio photograph 1997

Photo: Casey Orr
Black & white photographic print 92·5 × 91 cm

Occasionally Groovy

4 January 1997

Demonstration, Kunst und Teknik, Berlin.
Photo: Bam Hühnerkopf
Black & white photographic print 32 × 27·7 cm

Occasionally Groovy was a 12 inch record customised to produce sounds from both digital and analogue sources. Made by sticking a matt black template with holes cut out of it to the underside of a clear vinyl record the altered disc was placed onto a raised record deck with a light source comprising of a series of fairy-lights inserted beneath it.

A light sensor, attached to the arm of the record, produced sound as light passing through the record hit the sensor. Sound was also created in the normal manner of needle in groove. These two differing sources were played simultaneously: the sound of the original disco music on the record playing alongside the quickening rhythmic interruption of light hitting the sensor on the arm of the player.

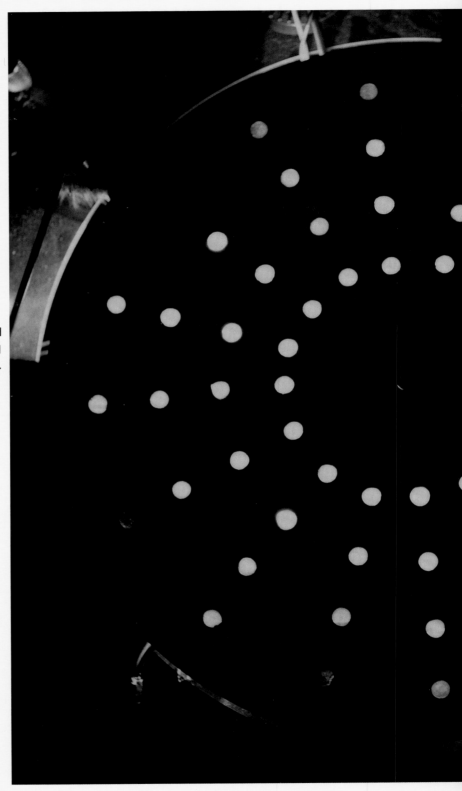

Pages 58–9

Bass in a Space

David Cunningham and Hayley
Newman, 15 March 1997

Studio Gallerie, Budapest.
Photo overleaf: Hayley Newman
Black & white photographic print 21 × 24 cm

A large PA system was placed in a small
room, playing back slowed down sound
containing frequencies as low as the
equipment would tolerate (the size of
the room was inversely proportional to
the size of the PA).

The crack in the wall appeared at
1·30pm, 3 hours and 30 minutes into installation time.

Exploding LEGO

1 September 1997

Oxford Street, London. Photo: Iris Garalf
Colour C-Type photographic print 50·5 × 76cm

I was asked to produce a musical event for the launch of the new radio station Xfm. I chose to work with the group London Electric Guitar Orchestra (LEGO) in organising a simultaneous busking event. During the event members of LEGO were asked to busk an identical song in unison with one another along the length of Oxford Street in London. Using radio transceivers and receivers to maintain contact with each other LEGO were placed at 30 metre intervals along the north side of Oxford Street, where they played an hour long concert.

Pedestrians experienced the concert as individual parts, walking in and out of the various sound fields as each busker they passed played a continuation of the segment that they had previously heard. The sound of the whole concert was assimilated and broadcast live on Xfm.

LEGO guitarists: John Bisset, Steve Mallaghan, Rick Nogalski, Ivor Kalim, Nigel Teers, Viv Doogan, Jorg Graumann, Richard Sanderson.

The Visit
11 October 1997

Rootless, Beverley. Photo: Casey Orr
Colour R-Type photographic print
16·5 × 11·5 cm

Wearing the world's first punk sleeping bag, I appeared 'hanging out' in and around Beverley, not doing anything in particular. The bag was covered in zips which allowed me to extend my arms and legs through its various orifices.

Over the day whilst inside the bag, I visited local shops to buy bread, cheese, fruit and soft drinks. At lunch time I opened up the sleeping bag, laid it out in the market square, had a picnic on it, read a book and then zipped myself up again.

Lock-jaw
Lecture Series
1997–1998

Lectures given at Chelsea College of Art,
Middlesex University, Sheffield & Hallam
University and Dartington College of Art.
Photo: Jonny Byars
Colour C-Type photographic print 17 × 25·5 cm

Over the period of a year I was invited
to give a series of lectures on my work.
Before each lecture I visited a local den-
tist and had my mouth anaesthetised.
With my mouth made immobile, I gave
my feeblest apologies to the students
and staff before attempting to talk on
my work.

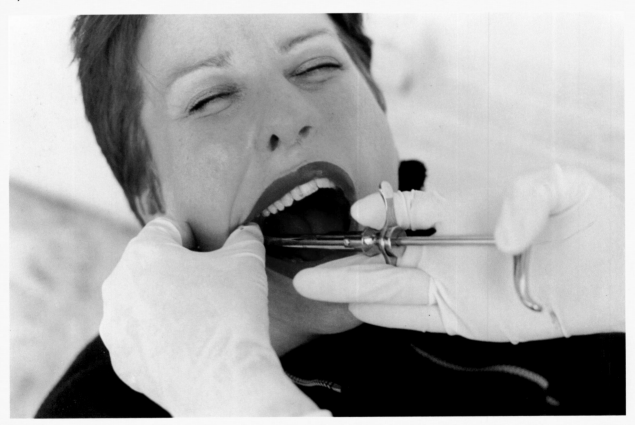

Human Resources

6 April 1998

Obero Offices, Montreal. Photo: Sylvie Gilbert
Colour R-Type photographic print 103 × 102 cm

Over a 9–5 working period I sat in the offices of Obero and captured my breathing in over 3,000 plastic sandwich bags. During the period, breaks totalling one and half-hours were taken for lunch and tea.

The work was an attempt to quantify and produce a visual record of the amount of breath breathed out during a working day.

Smoke, Smoke, Smoke

22 May 1998

Gallery Otto Plonk, Bergen.
Photo: Per-Gunner Tverbakk
Three black & white photographic prints
70·5 × 108 cm

Smoke, Smoke, Smoke was a silent choral work based on a series of pre-written scores and performed by a choir of invited musicians and sound artists. The piece uses the framework of a choir to present a primarily non-vocal work in which cigarette smoke was used to plot the tract of the voice. A conductor gave visual instructions to the choir, which they repeated simultaneously. Each passage performed was written to last the approximate length of time taken to smoke a cigarette.

Score no.1

This section to take place in the dark until instruction number 6

1 Light cigarettes in the dark.

2 Smoke slowly in synch following a metronomic rhythm.

3 Back row smoke in double time, two front rows smoke in metronomic time.

4 Back row smoke in quadruple time, middle row double, front row metronomic time.

5 Flick ash onto the floor.

6 As light slowly fades up, open mouths as if singing.

7 Blow smoke onto part of body of your choice.

8 Blow smoke onto part of neighbour's body.

9 Flick finished cigarette ends as high as possible into the air.

Choir: Alison Goldfrapp, Keiko Owada, Simon Fisher-Turner, Mitch, Miles Miles, Simon Woods, Hayley Newman, Bruce Gilbert, Gio D'Angelo, David Cunningham, Matt Tarr, Karen Mirza, Sean Roe, Kaffe Matthews, James Young, Steve Malaghan, Mike Sumpter.

Soloist: Charles Kriel

Conductor: David Crawforth

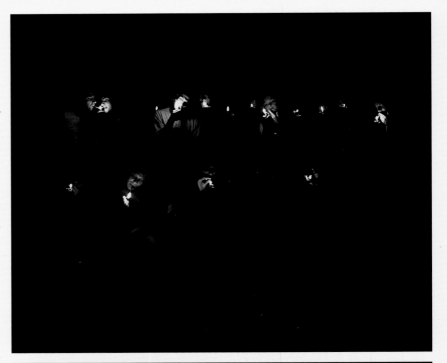

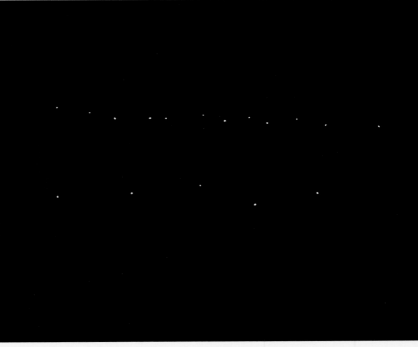

Football Audio Cup

21 June 1998

Shoreditch Biennial, London. Photos: Casey Orr
Nine colour C-Type photographic prints each
7·9 × 12·7cm

A reconstruction of the notorious
100th FA Cup final between Tottenham
Hotspur and Manchester City. The
match ended in a draw when
Manchester City's Tony Hutchinson
scored for both sides. The 1–1 draw
forced the first ever replay at Wembley.

    This reconstruction of the 1981 FA
Cup Final was replayed in real time using
a customised football and two teams.
During the game the players adhered to
and repeated the games events by following an audio recording of the
matches original radio commentary
which was playing back from within the
football itself.

Tottenham Hotspur: 1 L Price; 2 B Gilchrist;
3 G Newman; 4 K Reynolds; 5 L Taylor;
6 R Withers; 7 S Hart; 8 A Newman;
9 B Williams; 10 R Waring; 11 L Harvey

Manchester City: 1 J Bichard-Harding;
2 C Shillitoe; 3 S Cope; 4 R Silverman;
5 C Morgana; 6 Tinsey; 7 L Watts; 8 D Clegg;
9 D Guerro Miracle; 10 H Newman;
11 A Rachmatt

Referee: M Thompson

You Scratch Mine and I'll Scratch Yours

12 September 1998

Cyberia Café (as a part of digital summer 1998), Manchester. Photo: Lawrence Lane
Two colour C-Type photographic prints
40·5 × 40·5 cm

Durational 6 hour DJ-ing session with the lovely Matt (Stockhausen and Walkman) Wand. Within the six hour session of malarkey and frivolity Matt and I played golden oldies whilst covered in cobwebs and Christmas music with records embellished by snow.

Other activities included scratching with our right arms chained together, playing records with the needles covered with socks and promoting our new DJ-ing technique 'The knob' – a door knob stuck on the surface of the record to aid a more fluid scratching action.

Übertragung der Empfindungen der linken Hand in die Rechte
(A Translation of the Sensation of the Left Hand into the Right)

1999

I sit at a low table-like structure and place my left hand in a pat of butter. With my right hand I write about the sensations experienced by the fingers of the left hand encased within the butter.

A Translation of the Sensation of the Left Hand into the Right, 16 January 1999, 'Small Pleasures', 'Sensation', Hamburger Bahnhof, Berlin.

Photo: Mari Reijnders

(11) Hand has now moved down and the palm is in contact with the butter. Cold against warmth of the palm. The butter around the thumb has totally disintegrated, and the hand is almost in an horizontal position. The left side of the hand is still supported by a small mound of butter. Creamy. Dirty. Sort of thing you never normally get the chance to do.

Analogies? I don't know if there are any. Oh, theres that smell of butter again. Just wafted ~~past~~ past my

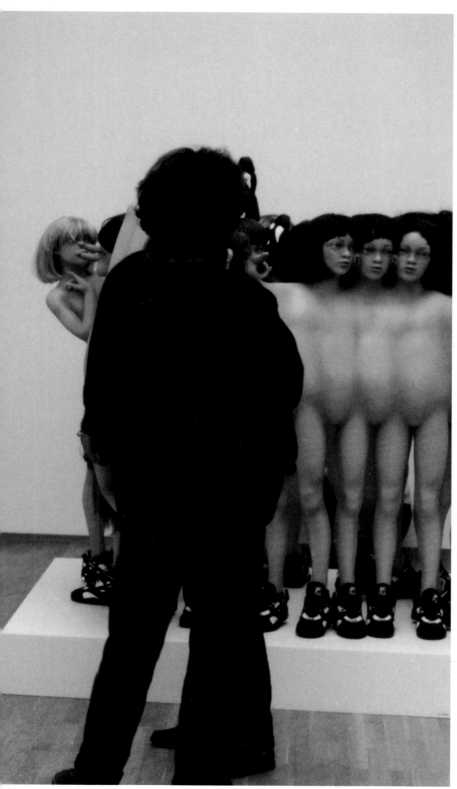

Kuß Prüfung (Kiss Exam)

1999

In *Kiss Exam* I perform kissing against a wall with a volunteer while attempting to write my consequent sensations on a pad mounted next to me.

Kiss Exam 16 January 1999, 'Small Pleasures', 'Sensation', Hamburger Bahnhof, Berlin.

Photo: Mari Reijnders

A simultaneous translation of the feeling of kissing into text.

I will try to describe the feelings of the kiss and my thoughts a different moments during the kiss. So from now on my thoughts will be transcribed as they happen. The performance will last for 1 hour.

The tongue is playing again teeth in small and deli... It is now playing with the his tongue. Suck lips my cheek. Groin against groin. breath in. Fish mouths again one and other. Tong inside my maybe my tong gxxe into his his nose us in my cheek because we are kissing to one side. hands on bottom (Right) lay at the absurdity. My eyes are going screwed and I cant feel the text any more. Its difficult to think while Kissing

KUB-PRüFUNG

pulling against two bodies. comfortable position. I don't want to write this any more. Just kiss. difficult to be cognitive where when you want to be able to move into your unconscious.

Suck tongue (mine) into his mouth. very soft. lips playing. end of tongues. open eyes. he's got blue eyes. tongues and spit.

Reposit. start straight on again. softly letting lips touch. I lick his lips. play with end of tongues. look into face. sweet kisses. Right arm around waist. left arm up on shoulder. stroking hair. pulling my buttocks into him. my left hand on his arm. not very romantic. move me to neck. such bother. lip.. I bite his lip. My left knee is in his groin twists to the side. bring leg (mine) over his left leg. stop. start again. softly moving tongues around

Sleepingbag/Postbag

1999

A sleeping bag with zips all over it. I lie inside the bag and write on postcards from the 'Sensation' exhibition itself as well as Post-it notes, stickers and paper. Once complete, I unzip the sleeping bag and 'post' the individual pieces of text out of the bag.

Sleepingbag/Postbag 16 & 17 January 1999, 'Small Pleasures', 'Sensation', Hamburger Bahnhof, Berlin.

Photo: Mari Reijnders

Smoke, Smoke, Smoke
1999

Smoke, Smoke, Smoke was a silent choral work for a choir that smokes. Initially presented in 1998 as a performance from the series *Connotations – Performance Images*, *Smoke, Smoke, Smoke* was realised in Cardiff, the land of the choir, during 1999.

Smoke, Smoke, Smoke 27 February 1999, Chapter Arts Centre, 'Cardiff Art in Time Festival', Cardiff.

Photo courtesy Cardiff Art and Time

Soundgaze
1999

Soundgaze is a performance in which two sets of electronic weighing scales are used to trigger over 300 sound samples. The objects used in the performance are organised according to their weight value and placed onto the scale. When on the scale, the weight values of these objects are sent as data to a piece of customised software on a computer which emits a sound from a corresponding file. Within the programme up to 400 sound samples may be ascribed to any weight value between 0·005kg and 150kg at increments of 0·005kg.

Soundgaze 23 October 1999, 'TOOT', Ferens Art Gallery, Hull; *Soundgaze*, 11 December 1999, 'Plopfizzbang', DIYplc, London; *Soundgaze* 20 February 2000, 'Audible Light', The Zodiac Club, Oxford; *Soundgaze* 15, 22 April & 13 May 2000, 'Beck's Futures', ICA, London; *Soundgaze* 19 May 2000, 'Performance Art in NRW 2000', Kunstraum, Düsseldorf; *Soundgaze* 26 May 2000, 'Performance Art in NRW 2000', Stadt Austellungshalle – Hawerkamp 22, Münster; *Soundgaze* 28 May 2000, 'Performance Art in NRW 2000', Maschinenhaus, Essen; *Soundgaze* 3 June 2000, 'Beck's Futures', Cornerhouse, Manchester; *Soundgaze* 23 March 2001, Preset, Nottingham.

Preliminary versions of *Soundgaze* performed at varying stages and with other titles: *10 Stone 12 Pounds* 19, 20 & 21 May, Cube, Manchester; *10 stone 12 pounds* 2–4 June, Muséet for Samtidskunst, Oslo. Version performed as *dr dr drumming* with Richard Hylton 4 September 1999, 'My Eye Hurts', The Green Room, Manchester and 12 September 1999, Threadwaxing Space, New York.

Photo courtesy ASA-European

Sucksniffdribble-scratch

1999

Sucksniffdribblescratch is a series of four works written as instruction for other people to perform. Taking place in a flat in the centre of Stockholm, some of the performances reflected domestic aspects of the flat that they took place in.

Instructions for spitting performance in bathroom

The performer wears a pair of radio headphones that relay specific instructions to spit all over a bathroom for one hour. The performer repeatedly fill's her mouth with water from a tap spitting it out over tiles and fittings in the room.

Instructions for making soup

Developed out of an earlier collaboration with the German artist Eike. Again in this work the performer wears a pair of radio headphones and is instructed to make soup using only her mouth. Carrying water in her mouth from the kitchen taps to the hob, the performer fills a series of pans. At a later stage vegetables were prepared by masticating food and spitting it out into the simmering pans.

My mannerisms

A performer opens 150 envelopes, each of which contains a hand-written letter instructing the performer's action. Based on descriptions of my own mannerisms, the consequent actions were slight and practically invisible.

Actions to be performed as quickly as possible

Wearing a pair of radio headphones the performer is instructed to carry out a series of rapid audio instructions as they are spoken.

Sucksniffdribblescratch, 20 November – 19 December 1999, 'Patentia', Drottinggatan 81, Stockholm.

Photos: Jan Hietala and Hayley Newman

Thinking

2000

A performance written to be performed by someone else as a first encounter.

Facing the audience, the performer sits next to a clock wearing a pair of headphones. A series of spoken thoughts the performer has not heard before are relayed over the phones. The seated audience is supplied with the text being spoken over the headphones including times at which the thoughts are being suggested. In this work, the performer is seen 'thinking' the suggested thoughts for the first time.

Thinking was performed by Caroline Achaintre, 20 May 2000, 'Point of view', Richard Salmon Gallery

Photo: Valerie Vivancos

Bubble

2000

A walk from my studio in the East End of London to the Lisson Gallery in the West.

On the evening of the opening of the exhibition I walked from my studio to the gallery wearing a new pair of shoes. On arrival I removed the shoes, sawed off their uppers and nailed the soles to the wall. I then titled, dated and signed the adjacent text panel.

Bubble 13 July 2000, 'A Shot in the Head', Lisson Gallery, London.

Photo: Aaron Williamson

The text panel for *Bubble* read:

[…] is a performance work that involves a walk between my studio in East London to the Lisson Gallery in the West wearing a brand new, previously unworn pair of shoes. Setting off at 3·30pm on 13 July 2000 the plan is to arrive at the Lisson Gallery's Summer Show opening at around 6·30pm, half an hour after the show has opened.

The shoes, which I intend to buy prior to the walk are the biggest worry. I want to buy a pair of shoes that are both elegant and comfortable and have a sole that is soft enough to scuff as a record of the journey. The marks picked up by the shoes attempting to offer an impression of the city that has attached itself to my walk. My speculation is that a pair of shoes with a leather sole would best suit the purpose. It is likely that I will set off with a handbag packed with plasters and a pair of socks in case the shoes hurt.

The walk traces the most direct route from my studio in Bethnal Green down the Bethnal Green Road to Old Street, up City Road to Islington and on to Kings Cross. From Kings Cross the route continues along Euston Road, which eventually becomes the Marylebone Road, near to the Lisson Gallery on Bell Street.

Upon arrival I will remove the shoes, saw the soles off and display them as an art exhibit. This work will be titled after the model of shoe I eventually choose to buy and walk in.

Wrapping
2000
Controlling volume by wrapping objects that make sound.

Wrapping, 20 September 2000, 'Quiet', Bar Centro, Manchester.

Photo: Matt Wand

Here/There

In collaboration with
The Mixed Reality Laboratory
at The University of Nottingham
2000
A performance for children using the
virtual reality software KidStory. Based
on a system in which barcode tags were
used to 'call up' images the performance
linked an object to its screen-based representation, attributing multiple associations to individual articles. A potato,
scanned in on three different occasions
appeared as an image of a pile of crisps,
a bowl of mash and in the action of
being peeled.

Here/There 27 October 2000,
'Kids@NOWfestival', Royal Albert Hall,
Nottingham.

Photo: Holly Fowke

The Daily Hayley
2001

A series of performances that are intended to take place over 16 days. Based on a six month collection of newspapers spanning the first half of 2001, the performances in *The Daily Hayley* will use the newspaper archive as source material for a series of works presented in the exhibition.

The Daily Hayley, 15–30 September 2001, Matt's Gallery, London.

Photo (work in progress): Hayley Newman

Hayley Newman Self-Interview

h The interview as a format is similar to that of a performance in that, once beyond the moments of conduction, it occupies a space in the past. A performance, like an interview, is an event that can be experienced within either a primary or, if any form of documentation is available, a secondary context, as either a present or a past actuality.

H In contrast to a performance, however, the interview is an occasion in which the document is an intrinsic element of the event as well as its by-product. This particular self-interview is happening at a slower pace than a normal conversation; it is a considered, explicit construct and so may be read as a performance in its own right. The audience in this particular situation is addressed as readers rather than as listeners or viewers.

You talk about your readers as being similar to an audience; can you explain more about the relationship between the terms 'readers' and 'audience'?

The notion of readers as audience is posited intentionally in order to identify this text as a temporal event with performative conditions where the interview, whilst being read as a document of a past event, represents the 'live' quality of the original spoken word. The term 'performative' is used to encompass expanded notions of performance and to suggest acts that are either located or received, or have the potential to be located or received, within a physical context. **By identifying the device of the interview as a temporal rather than a definitive structure, this self-interview positions its readers in a way that is similar to their forming an audience. The 'liveness' of the source allows its audience to accept inaccuracy and deviance, it being a temporal act that has only solidified as a gesture made to the future.**

Whilst constructing the text I am predicting responses to its content, structure and the way it is written by this imagined audience. I am shaping the text anticipating some sort of effect or result and am projecting my thoughts to a future moment beyond my presence, to a time in which this text will be re-activated through being read. The self-interview presented as a performance within the frame of this page, may therefore be seen as the document of an event, positing its readers as audience in an attempt to circumvent its own corporeality.

In characterising this interview as a performance and its readers as an audience, how then is your identity as a performer formed within the conversation presented here on the page?

As stated earlier, this self-interview presented here on the page performs in an imagined time and place outside the encounter of reading. In actuality, there are factors occurring beyond this page whilst writing this text that the audience is not witness to. I could be writing this at home, on a beach, in a studio, a library or a bed, alternatively I may be wearing a pair of lucky shoes, a man's suit, a chicken costume, or be on a summer holiday in Ireland. The content, tone, gesture and expression of the text shapes my identity as an author whilst my personal identity masquerades behind the fictional improvisation of a real-time discussion played out through the instruments of the interviewer and interviewee. This masquerade plays upon the conclusion of the text being read. As with a performance that sometimes appears spontaneous and unplanned, it has in fact been

carefully staged. The strain of the work process is eradicated or disguised through a highly particular and meticulous approach to writing.

As with other performance works, my identification as the performer is defined through the context or medium chosen for the event. In the self-interview, the dynamic of the traditional interview is replaced by the binary of performer/audience. The 'selfhood' of the performer is performed to this (imaginary) audience directly through the form of the interview.

How then did this transition between writing as a form of reflection after a performance move into thinking about writing as performance?

The transition between writing as a form of reflection and writing as performance happened relatively quickly, spurred on by the invitation to do a series of performances in the 'Sensation' exhibition at the Hamburger Bahnhof in Berlin in 1999. A combination of pragmatic decisions brought about by limited budgets and practical commitments led to three performances; *Kiss Exam*, *A Translation of the Sensation of the Left Hand into the Right* and *Sleepingbag/Postbag*. All of the cited works were located amongst the exhibits in the 'Sensation' exhibition at the Hamburger Bahnhof in Berlin. *Kiss Exam* took place next to the Chapman Brother's sculpture *Zygotic Acceleration* (1995), *A Translation of the Sensation of the Left Hand into the Right* was performed opposite *Text Painting* (1995) by Peter Davies whilst *Sleepingbag/Postbag* occurred next to the work *Au Naturel* (1994) by Sarah Lucas. In all three of these performances I attempted to write about an activity simultaneous to performing it. In *Kiss Exam* I perform kissing against a wall with a volunteer whilst attempting to write my consecutive sensations on a pad mounted to the wall next to me. The producer of the 'Small Pleasures' event Mattias Osterwold and myself approached an architectural assistant in a Berlin bar a couple of nights before the performance and asked if he would be my kissing partner in a performance at the Hamburger Bahnhof. As I kiss the stranger, I write a description of the kiss. Likewise in *A Translation of the Sensation of the Left Hand into the Right* I sit at a low table-like structure and place my left hand in a pat of butter. With my right hand I write about the sensations experienced by the fingers of the left hand engulfed by the butter. The texts for both *Kiss Exam* and *A Translation …* use the present tense to directly link the moments of action to its writing whilst the length of both texts were determined by the one-hour duration of the performances.

In *Sleepingbag/Postbag* I lie on the floor inside a customised sleeping bag. A series of smaller zips sewn into the bag allows me to open the bag from inside and 'post' the postcards, stickers, Post-it notes and sheets of paper I write on during the performance outside of the bag.

In choosing the title *A Translation of the Sensation of the Left Hand into the Right* you must have been conscious of the wordplay between the use of the adjective 'right' and the verb 'to write' which, when pronounced, only distinguish themselves from one another through their context?

Yes, I was conscious of the interchangeable meaning of both titles, even though the titles for *Kiss Exam* and *A Translation …* were originally written in German. The German translation of *Kiss Exam* is *Kuß Prüfung*, whilst *A Translation of the Sensation of the Left Hand into the Right* reads as *Übertragung der Empfindungen der linken Hand in die Rechte*.

I am right-handed, so describing the activity of writing with my right hand was literal in both English and German. Both *Kiss Exam* and *A Translation …* follow a similar format: that of assimilating writing into the performance by the subjective articulation of the performer's experience during the event. In *A Translation …* the performance traces tactile information experienced by the left hand up the left arm into the brain where it is made conscious before being articulated into muscular activity in the right arm and subsequently hand in order to be expressed into text.

In *A Translation …* I remain seated, whereas *Kiss Exam* is performed standing up. By performing the work whilst standing, I intended to place the resulting description within the oracular tradition of speech in which public speaking is normally conducted standing up. But whereas in a public address the mouth is normally used to speak, in this instance it is used to kiss. As my mouth responds physically to the kisser, my hand articulates the transformation of the sensation of kissing into text.

In the performance *Sleepingbag/Postbag* I lie on the gallery floor and post the texts outside the bag. The hand used to write the text privately inside the sleeping bag is the same hand that delivers the text to its audience outside the bag.

It seems to me that the hand plays alternative roles in each of the performances. In **Kiss Exam**, the mouth occupied with the act of kissing devolves the articulation of the encounter to the hand, which in turn writes rather than speaks of its experience. In **A Translation …** the left hand is a receptor, receiving stimuli, whilst the right hand is the mechanism through which this information is transposed into text. In **Sleepingbag/ Postbag** however, the act of writing on postcards inside the sleeping bag remains obscured and the hand is only seen as it emerges from the bag to deliver the text to its audience.

The text for the work was written during the performance on a pad of A4 paper placed on the wall next to you in pink and red felt-tip pen. Does this have a special significance? And what about the emphasis on handwriting in the other performances?

The choice of the pink and red pens reflects the colours of the mouth, whilst the lined paper relates to the linear constraints of writing whilst kissing. My writing starts off neatly, following the ruled lines on the page. As I succumb to the physical sensations of the performance my writing becomes unruly, almost illegible, slipping beyond the confines of the space delineated for writing. The writing thereby not only communicates a physical response to the kiss in its content but also in the expression of the handwriting on the page. As body language is used to emphasise meaning in speech, the quality of my handwriting in *Kiss Exam* provides information that enhances the reading of the work.

The text for *A Translation …* however, was written on green and yellow paper, reflecting the visual properties common to packaged butter. Unlike with *Kiss Exam*, the handwriting in this performance is controlled and neat, reflecting its more meditative character.

The performance **A Translation …** makes me think of scientific methodology in which an experiment is recorded through the observation of one or more factors. In the writing you describe the sensation of the hand in the butter and what it looks like as well as supplying an initial paragraph describing your intention within the work. You also contextualise the work as a live performance by referring in the text to two people who are present documenting the work as well as a member of the audience.

In **Kiss Exam**, you also outline your intent and contextualise the writing by referencing the location of the work. However, what I essentially find interesting in this text is that the direct documentation of an intimate experience, which may normally be recorded after the event in a diary or similar device, happens here in a public frame. This immediate expression of the intimate experience of a kiss makes reading the text awkward and places the reader in an uncomfortable and voyeuristic position. Whereas an entry in a diary is written in private, solely for the eyes of its author, the text of **Kiss Exam** was written in public. Alongside **A Translation ...** this text has subsequently been made into an artist's book. The two books titled *Kiss* and *Butter* were made in 1999 for the project DOT which was curated by Elizabeth Price and hosted as an ongoing archive of artists' work in our studio at 5 Teesdale Yard, E2, from the 1 April 1999 until the 30 March 2000.

After the event, the books allow both myself and the reader to witness the experience of performing made explicit within the moments of corporeal action documented during the event of the work itself. Such writings present a way of documenting work from within, allowing a more direct relationship between the practical and textual investigations and the role that documentation plays in the retrospective consolidation of a performance as a temporal activity.

As objects, the original hand-written texts are artefacts and represent a physical link to the time of performing. The sheets of paper are the remains of an activity which crease, fade and discolour with proportional relation to the past event and present/future moment. Hence the text unites the sensation of performing with the attempt to drag the moment of performing into a later consciousness, an *impasse* activity. This is particularly apparent in my experience of performing *Kiss Exam* in which the struggle to articulate sensation was challenged by my growing desire to 'abandon' myself to a kiss.

The documents give varying insights and ways of reading the performance works presented through them. The stillness of the exterior performance image is represented as a photograph whilst the flux of the interior performance experience is presented as text.

In all these instances your position as a writer is located between an imagined fantasy of the act of writing and an exploration of the medium of writing in relation to a performance. The interplay between fiction, fantasy and textual convention is also explored in the work **Connotations – Performance Images**. *Connotations – Performance Images* (originally titled *Connotations – Performance Images 1994–98*) was initially presented as a retrospective exhibition of performance works from the period 1994–98, (*Connotations – Performance Images 1994–98*, 10–25 October 1998, Beverley Art Gallery, Beverley) and included textual and photographic documentation of 21 performances I did not make. Can you say something about this work?

With *Connotations* ... I began to think about the conventions of text within the *oeuvre* of performance documentation. Looking specifically at the conventional book format used for the distribution of performance work, I selected texts that artists had written in the 1970s to describe their performances. Within the conceptual artworks of that period I identified a common trajectory in which the performance was developed from an idea on paper through to realisation, before being returned to a paper format through photographic and textual description.

This trajectory follows the stages; plan – performance – document. Many actions undertaken by this generation of artists, being led by conceptual ideas, lent themselves to description in text, thereby making them ideal for the double documentation of image and text. In this construction the text was a document often written after the event, which, composed in the first-person past participle, was considered to be a record of an action, just as the photograph was a document. I noticed that these texts combined specific circumstantial details such as date, time, place and duration with a description of the event and personal recount in order to expand the information presented in the image. The conceptual nature of much of the work described in this way is represented in texts often no longer than a paragraph in length.

In a sense, the mechanics of performance practice from this period corroborate its position within a conceptual frame. The significance of such works from the 1970s can be seen as relative to a synthesis of concept and performance, which is reflected in artist's descriptions of such works. Accounts written by Abramović and Ulay for example emphasise the conceptual nature of their work by identifying individual roles within the performance but without conveying their individual experiences of performing. There are three different ways in which they describe their work: some of their texts use the plural voice 'we', describing the mirrored action of both parties in a performance, whilst in others they use the first person singular 'I' in conjunction with either the name Marina or Ulay. The texts that use the first person singular give voice to both Marina and Ulay as individual collaborators, either duplicating their experience of the performance with both Abramović and Ulay relaying the same performance descriptions, or by emphahsising the different roles undertaken by each artist in the work. Three different examples of Abramović & Ulay's texts relating to their collaborative performance works.

AAA–AAA

In a given space.

Performance.

We are facing each other, both producing a continuous vocal sound.

We slowly build up the tension, our faces coming closer together until we are screaming into each other's open mouths.

Duration: 15 minutes.

February 1978, RTB television studio, Liège, Belgium. Performed for television.

March 1978, Amsterdam. Performed for film.

Relation to Movement

In a chosen space.

Performance.

Ulay

I am driving the car for an indefinite time in a circle.

Marina

I am sitting in the car, moving for an indefinite time in a circle, announcing the number of circles by megaphone.

Duration: 16 hours

September 1977, 10me Biennale de Paris. Visitors: 200.

Interruption in Space

The given space is divided by a wall into two equal parts.

Performance.

Marina

I am walking towards the wall.

I walk towards the wall touching it with my body.

I run towards the wall hitting it with my body.

Ulay

I am walking towards the wall.

I walk towards the wall touching it with my body.

I run towards the wall hitting it with my body.

Duration: 46 minutes

January 1977, Kunstakademie 'Rinke Klasse', Düsseldorf. Visitors: 120.

From: Marina Abramović, *Artists Body*, with texts by Marina Abramović, Toni Stooss, Thomas McEvilley, Bojana Pejji, Hans

Ulrich Obrist, Chrissie Iles, Jan Avgikos. Thomas Wullfen, Velimir Abramović, Edizioni Charta, 1998, *AAA–AAA* p.184, *Relation*

in Movement p.162, *Interruption in Space* p.142.

The text panels for *Connotations* … **were written after having observed the often matter-of-fact style used by Chris Burden whilst recounting his own perform-ances, whilst one of the Connotations pieces** *B(in)* **was loosely based on** *Deadman,* **one of Burden's actions from the 1970s.** The text for *B(in)* states that I spend the day inside a bin bag in New York waiting for the garbage men to pick me up and that when they arrive I jump out of the bag and run home. The work itself, initially a resolution of an idea to make a performance inside a bin bag is also a comment on or re-negotia-tion of Burden's performance *Deadman* in which, hidden beneath a canvas tarpaulin on La Cienega Boulevard in Los Angeles, Burden puts both himself and drivers in danger by becoming unrecognisable as a living human form. Burden's work resolves itself when the police arrive and arrest him for 'causing a false emergency to be reported' (see *Deadman* description below). In *B(in)* I remain hidden and like Burden use a material and location to hide within that may be associ-ated with death. However, Burden's work presented an immediate physical danger from the passing cars on the freeway whilst mine proposed minimal potential danger in the form of bin men arriving and placing me in the back of a garbage truck. *B(in)* ends when, as the bin men approach, I claim to run home away from the danger, puncturing the heroism of Burden's arrest.

Burden's description of *Deadman* read as follows:

Deadman

12 November 1972, Riko Mizuno Gallery, Los Angeles, California

At 8pm I lay down on La Cienega Boulevard and was covered completely with a canvas tarpaulin. Two fifteen minute flares were placed near me to alert cars. Just before the flares extinguished, a police car arrived. I was arrested and booked for causing a false emergency to be reported. Trial took place in Beverly Hills. After three days of deliberation, the jury failed to reach a decision.

Chris Burden, Blocnotes Editions, 1995. **Burden's use of language in his descriptions can be seen as similar to the visual information presented in the photographic documenta-tion of some of the works. For example, in the photograph for the performance** *747* **we see Burden with his back to the viewer, holding a gun which he points up-wards at the sky in the direction of a Boeing 747. This image is extended through a single sentence that describes how Burden had shot at a Boeing 747 aeroplane** Burden's description of *747* read as follows:

747

5 January 1973, Los Angeles, California

At about 8am at a beach near the Los Angeles International Airport, I fired several shots with a pistol at a Boeing 747.

Chris Burden, Blocnotes Editions, 1995.

It seems as if the cool detachment of the text copies the factual authority of the camera in its documentation of the work, thereby acknowledging the difficulty of reproducing tone, cadence or emphasis in written language.

In playing down both the extraordinary physical feats and emotional content of his performances, the prosaic nature of Burden's texts limit our view of the work. This implies that any readings of the texts and images must be made through the work's absence.

Yes, I agree. Considering the oblique nature of such documentary evidence, the question occurred to me: 'how do we know that Burden performed this or any other of his works such as *Deadman*? ' **Again, the photographic documentation of this particular performance shows a close-up of what may be a body covered by a dark blanket de-marcated by two flares with a moving or parked car in the background. The video document of this piece is a wobbly film of two light blobs on a dark screen with Burden's voice introducing the performance video, apologising about the bad quality of the image. I am not suggesting that this performance did not happen but that a visual document (video/photograph) and text (speech/writing) are being used to authorise one another and that in their collusion they are self-reflexive.**

Perhaps this is similar to the convention in mass-media by which a photo is validated by a caption explaining the image or where a caption makes sense only in relation to its counterpart image.

Yes, precisely. Outside the actual performances these text/image documents from the 1970s appear to attempt self-reflexivity and seem to replace the action. The structure of the text/image based work *Connotations* … **follows or imitates these conventions of performance description from the 1970s in trying to 'authenticate' a series of fictional performances. Writing in the past tense and using the first person and providing background information such as date, time, place, photographer's name and title of the work, the texts also describe action and (occasionally) the consequences of that action. In making** *Connotations* …, **I was aware of how the image and the text in this sense sustain each other's narrative.**

In his essay for the *Out of Actions* catalogue, Guy Brett discusses the issue that performance is an area of practice in which no-one can be a specialist since it is impossible to have seen all performance work in its primary form. Guy Brett, *Out of Actions, Between Performance and the Object*, Thames & Hudson, 1998. Guy Brett's essay 'Life strategies: overview and selection' starts on p.197. The problem of not seeing work in its primary form, but instead considering secondary published material, such as a photograph with its supporting text, creates a vacuum that is often filled by anecdote and mythology. Is this phenomenon an aspect of **Connotations** … conception?

The individual pieces in this series rely on the interplay traditionally set up between text and image within performance documentation, reflecting the responsibilities and limitations of documenting the complexities of a 'real' event. In providing no information beyond the basic conceptual outline for the performance, the texts actively encourage the generation of anecdotes in their repetition and acceptance as documentation, or as truth.

I used text in a different way in *Bubble*. **For that performance the text was sent to the gallery before the opening and as all possible information about the work was**

contained within this text panel for the exhibit, no other description of intent or outline of the project was needed. *Bubble* was performed on 13 July 2000 as part of the exhibition 'A Shot in the Head' at the Lisson Gallery in London.

For the performance I walked from my studio in the East-End of London to the Lisson Gallery in the West, wearing a brand new pair of shoes. Upon arrival at the gallery I removed the shoes, sawed off the uppers and nailed the soles flat to the wall next to the mounted text. In hindsight, the text is similar to a proposal in that it both orientates intention whilst at the same time acknowledging the evolution of certain changes demanded by making work in practice. Within this text I provided the same kind of information as in those for *Connotations* … , such as date, location, time and description of the performance whilst at the same time allowing the speculative nature of its planning and realisation to be revealed through the body of the text's prediction. In this way and by the use of the predictive future tense, the text attempts to avoid the stasis that characterises written documentation on past events, since it is unable to reflect on or even describe the performance's own closure or conclusion. Through only offering a forecast, the text is neither reflection nor instruction and so disrupts the sequence of plan – performance – document that I had identified as the salient characteristic of performance documentation in the 1970s. The fact that the text for *Bubble* was written in the future tense before the event as both a script and a prediction of the performance's outcome was an attempt to bypass any confusion on the part of the press, which had occurred with the fake testimonies of *Connotations* … that had been shown in London just before *Bubble* was exhibited.

In **Bubble** the shoe-soles offer a physical record of the activity of walking from your studio in the East End of London to the gallery in the West End, literally tracing the transportation and delivery of an art object. The text for **Bubble** was completed when you arrived at the gallery by filling in the title of the work and then signing and dating the panel, thereby completing its prediction. (The title **Bubble**, was the name of the style of shoe that was used to walk from your studio to the gallery: an indeterminate factor when the text was completed). How do you see the role of the text more generally in relation to its status as art product or commodity?

By choosing to sign the text and not the shoes I reattribute its role and transform it from information panel to document, both making the performed action explicit and acknowledging the fulfilment of the prediction. As with the accounts in *Connotations* … the text-panel for *Bubble* is an integral part of the artwork and attributes the authorship of the textual information to the artist rather than to the anonymity of the institution. In contrast, the experiences written about during *Kiss Exam* and *A Translation* … occupy a different temporal space than the descriptions in both *Connotations* and *Bubble*. The manuscripts for *Kiss Exam* and *A Translation* … were produced within public situations and used the present tense to describe the immediacy of thoughts and emotions experienced during the performance. This made the process of documenting structurally intrinsic to the moments of the performance since physical experiences were being transformed 'live' into text.

However, similarly to *Connotations* … and *Bubble*, the texts for *Kiss Exam* and *A*

Translation … **operate simultaneously as both artefact and document. As artefact, they might be valued as an object through the means of their production and the circumstances of their origination, but they may also be seen as documents integral to the conceptual nature of the work. In this sense they follow the sequence plan – performance – document and yet still disrupt this trajectory by placing the document within the performance rather than in an external position before or after the event.** This self-interview has been extracted from Hayley Newman's unpublished doctoral thesis *Locating performance: Textual Identity and the Performative*, University of Leeds, 2001.

Performancemania has been produced on the occasion of Hayley Newman's exhibition 'The Daily Hayley' at Matt's Gallery, London. Saturday 15 – Sunday 30 September 2001

This publication has been financially assisted by Artsadmin from whom Hayley Newman received a bursary; The Arts Council of England, National Visual Arts Publishing Awards 2001/02; and Chelsea College of Art & Design, where Hayley Newman is a lecturer in the Fine Art Media Department.

The exhibition has been generously supported by The Henry Moore Foundation and was realised with a Commissioning Grant from the Combined Arts Department at London Arts.

Robin Klassnik wishes to thank the Matt's Gallery Committee – Scott Blyth, Patricia Bickers, Stephen Bury, Alan Haydon, Daphne Hyman, Henry Meyric Hughes and Avis Newman – for their support and advice; Ben Craze; Gerrie van Noord; FNJ Newsagent, Stepney; Hayley Newman; Aaron Williamson; and Sarah den Dikken for her continuous back-up and support.

Gallery interns: Sarah Grainger-Jones, Rosalind Horne, Alison Kibbey.

Special thanks to Andrew Wilson for his advice on the essays for this book.

Hayley Newman wishes to thank Artsadmin; Phil Baines; Sarah den Dikken; Robin Klassnik; Nina Könnemann; Jacqueline Newman; Casey Orr; Aaron Williamson; and Andrew Wilson.

Hayley Newman and Matt's Gallery would also like to extend their thanks to the students who volunteered to work in the gallery with the artist throughout July and August, during her research and preparation for 'The Daily Hayley'. From Chelsea College of Art & Design: Jeff Lee, Chris McCormack, Terry McCormack, Natascha Ochel, Eleanora Rosatone and Stephan Takkides; from Kingston University: Barbara McQuillan; from Central Saint Martins College of Art & Design: Seraina Müller; from Slade School of Art: Naoko Takahashi; from Goldsmiths' College: Hiroaki Enoki and Mario Schruff. Genevieve Kalnins. Thanks to Verena Jabs for making the wardrobe for the artist's performances, and Mariana Ziadeh for documenting the performances throughout the 16 day run – both from Chelsea College of Art & Design.

Commissions

Ecomiss was commissioned by Public Art Development Trust on behalf of *The Economist Magazine* for 'The Economist Ninth Annual Summer Exhibition' 1994.

Microphone Skirt was commissioned by Osterwalder's Art Office on the occasion of the exhibition 'Im Pure', 1995.

Rude Mechanic was commissioned in collaboration with David Crawforth by The Arts Council of England for Beaconsfield, 1996.

Crystalline I was commissioned by Norwich Art Gallery, 1997.

Connotations – Performance Images 1994–98 was comissioned by Hull Time Based Arts, 1998.

Smoke, Smoke, Smoke was commissioned by Cardiff Art and Time, 1999.

Soundgaze was commissioned in two phases: the first phase of commissioning was supported by Work and Leisure International, whilst the second phase was made whilst Newman was Arts Council of England Live Artist-in-Residence on the Phonic Art BA at the University of Lincolnshire & Humberside, 1999.

Sucksniffdribblescratch was commissioned by Jan Heitäla/NIFCA for the exhibition 'Patentia', 1999.

Here/There was commissioned by the NOW Festival, Nottingham in collaboration with The University of Nottingham, 2000.

Designed and typeset in Gill Sans by Phil Baines

1,000 copies printed and bound by specialblue, London

Copy editor: Gerrie van Noord

'The Daily Hayley' exhibition has been supported by the following British newspapers:

THE ARTS COUNCIL OF ENGLAND

The Henry Moore Foundation

LONDON ARTS

THE LONDON INSTITUTE
Chelsea College of Art & Design

artsadmin